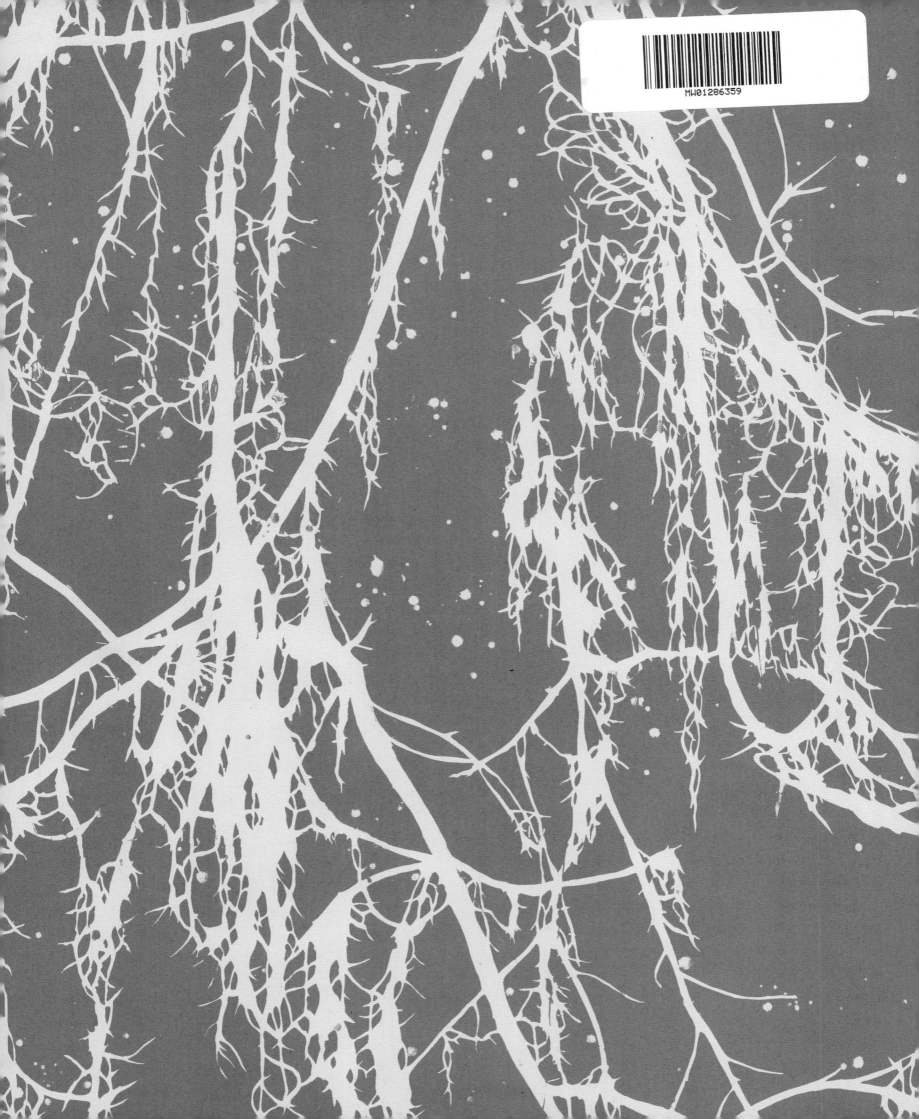

EMBRACING BEAUTY

To my family, who are my true home.

Contents

INTRODUCTION *8*

A PLACE OF TRANQUILITY AND GRACE *12*

OUTSIDE OF TIME *46*

COASTAL LIGHT *72*

A GROUNDED SPIRIT *92*

A DREAM THE SEA MAKES *110*

SOLIDITY AND STRENGTH *126*

A STUDY IN CLARITY *152*

A STORYBOOK MADE REAL *168*

CREATIVITY IN DIALOGUE *202*

ELEGANCE AND REPOSE *226*

ORDER, PEACE, AND HARMONY *252*

SANCTUARY *270*

ACKNOWLEDGMENTS *286*

PROJECT CREDITS *287*

Introduction

Sanctuary is a form of embrace. When you imbue a home with warmth, welcome, charm, and ease, it holds you in return—a room becomes a refuge, a house a haven. As a designer, it is my life's work to achieve this with each and every project. I want a home to be well-designed, I want it to be beautiful, but more than anything I want it to provide peace. To be a place of connection and embrace.

With that purpose, I strive to design serene interiors that bring joy to the families that inhabit them—places where a good life can unfold. We design with serene palettes and rich textures. We choose furnishings with comfort and presence. We select artwork and antiques with soul and patina. Each meticulous step is a true labor of love on the journey to creating spaces in which peace and joy can unfold, in which memory and meaning will deepen over time.

As interior designers and architects, we are very fortunate to be able to see and feel rooms in our heads before they are ever built. It is a gift and one I do not take for granted. We listen carefully to those who entrust their homes to us as they describe their hopes, wishes, and dreams, and we envision and feel what they describe. We then strive to deliver exactly that, while hopefully exceeding expectations.

In my first book, *An Eye for Beauty*, I explored how the senses help to create sanctuary—how light and color, texture, sound, and scent influence our environments. From the way the local light interacts with a palette—and how the subtlest difference in shade can transform the feeling of a space—to the touch of a textile so soft that it elicits an immediate sense of calm. A deeply attentive choreography of these elements enables the whole to be much more than the sum of its parts. It creates atmosphere.

In *Embracing Beauty*, we share twelve projects where this is exquisitely realized. We travel from a Jackson Hole residence with an organic materiality that is both rustic and refined to a grand, gabled Kiawah Island retreat on the edge of the Atlantic. From a stunning modernist Alys Beach home to my own Buckhead pied-à-terre, where classicism and comfort mingle.

Elsie de Wolfe's guiding principle, "I am going to make everything around me beautiful—that will be my life," is much quoted but resonates in all I do from start to finish, beginning to end. The foundation of this philosophy is to make it an intentional daily practice—to actively embrace beauty. Whether you choose to express it in art, tabletop, culinary expertise, floral arrangements, or gardening, each pursuit of beauty cultivates our physical and emotional well-being. Embracing beauty, in whatever form we choose, elevates our lives.

I often am asked what's the best part of what we do, and the answer is simple: the days we introduce our wonderful clients to their beautiful new homes. When they walk in, on nearly every occasion, there are tears of joy on both our parts. I do what I do with passion because I care as deeply about how a house *feels* as how it lives and looks. Because the work is truly from the heart.

A Place of Tranquility and Grace

A pale wool sateen drapes from a canopy. A bedframe floats, suspended from the ceiling by slender chains. This lightness of touch defines the soul of this house, a residence for which elegance was the impetus and sanctuary the aspiration. It began with the brilliant client, an entrepreneur whose vitality, energy, and decisiveness built her thriving company, and who brought all of these marvelous qualities to the design process. When she acquired this Tennessee River residence, it had beautiful structure and grounds, but its interiors were dark, weighted down by heavy wood finishes. The client commissioned architect D. Stanley Dixon, who elevates everything he touches, to transform it into a place of tranquility and grace. She put her trust in him and in my firm and gave us creative carte blanche.

Stan and I dedicated ourselves to releasing the house into light. He opened the rooms brilliantly, and we channeled that illumination into a subtle spectrum for the overall palette. We brought microscopic attention to the nuancing of pigments to make the house feel as soft and sublime as it does. The extraordinary quality of light enabled perception of the subtlest shades and details: the sand-and-cream tracery of the Mansour rug, the whispered tone of the Jamb stone mantel, the pearlescent shell-gray of a bowl. The house is a palimpsest of quiet hues, like layer upon layer of Japanese rice paper.

This luminous atmosphere was a dream setting for art. It's a particular privilege and joy for me to work with a client to curate a meaningful collection. I began my career as a private art dealer, and my many years spent immersed in

PREVIOUS PAGE: A textural composition in the living room anchored by Maysey Craddock's *Vessel for a Rising Sun* (2022), a mixed-media work in gouache, thread, and flashe on found paper. Before the piece stands a Tang dynasty horse atop a midcentury French oak buffet. In the foreground, a luxurious silk mohair wraps the custom sofa. OPPOSITE AND FOLLOWING PAGES: Above the carved Portland stone Jamb chimneypiece in the living room is a meditative oil on paper by Callum Innes from the artist's 2015 *Cento* series. It quietly, yet powerfully, centers the room.

museums and galleries informs everything I do. Here, we had the opportunity to acquire works by contemporary painters, photographers, and sculptors and place them in dialogue with existing pieces. Works by artists such as Callum Innes, Janaina Tschäpe, and Yumiko Utsu now occupy the home alongside pieces by de Kooning, Matisse, and Picasso. One of my favorite moments is in the great room, where above the mantel an abstract by Innes emanates quiet presence. Innes is an artist who shares my interest in the interrelation of positive and negative space, and I always find his color studies meditative and moving.

The project was graced by the presence of another artist—the landscape architect Stephen W. Hackney. Stephen has exquisite taste—he sees with a classicist's eye but always draws deeply on the genius of place. He composed every inch of the property, designing everything from formal dining gardens to sweeping lawns. The partnership between Stephen and the client turned out to be inspired on all fronts. They would ultimately discover in each other kindred spirits, and, in a magical denouement, the completion of the house dovetailed with their marriage. They celebrated with a reception at their new home.

Late in his life, the painter Giorgio Morandi, that master of the tranquil hue, wrote, "My only ambition is to enjoy the peace and quiet which I require in order to work." Our driven client is known to be up every day at four a.m., so delivering a space of respite and refuge for her was very important to me. She has since shared that she is so in love with her bedroom that on the weekends she now sleeps in until nine.

OPPOSITE: In the softly illuminated foyer, graceful sculptural pieces set the serene tone of the home. FOLLOWING PAGES: With its air of easy elegance, the dining room can host relaxed or formal gatherings; the undulating lines of the lanterns and the drape of the skirted, wool-satin dining chairs add a romantic dimension.

ABOVE, LEFT TO RIGHT: Punctuating the hallway that connects the foyer to the living room is *Palimpseste* (1966), a mixed-media work by French artist Georges Noël, above a bronze stool. Hervé van der Straeten's transfixing Branches mirror unfurls above an antique Italian demilune. A vignette of curvilinear objects atop an oak credenza with panels of pierced interlace carving. A lyrical Ellsworth Kelly lithograph, *Calla Lily II* (1983-1985), captures the essential lines of flowers.

PREVIOUS PAGES, ABOVE, AND OPPOSITE: The kitchen's many textures—woven-seagrass counter stools, plaster pendants, handmade tiles, and Calacatta Violette marble—can be appreciated in detail in this always-luminous space. A sheer linen curtain wall separates the dining room and kitchen. The all-white palette of the architectural details, cabinetry, and tile gives a harmonious foundation to the space.

OPPOSITE: In the keeping room we created an intimate arrangement with shapely, low-back lounge chairs, leather-cushioned benches, and a trayed ottoman in lieu of a table. The focal point is an art installation layering *Oiseau No. 82* (1963) by Picasso with *Hummingbird* (2022) by Shelley Reed, an artist who works exclusively in black and white. *Florentine* (1938) by Henri Matisse gracefully punctuates the setting.

PREVIOUS PAGES: Designed to be a sanctuary for our clients, the primary bedroom is a luxurious haven, from the headboard upholstered in white cashmere to the virgin wool–wrapped chaise. ABOVE, LEFT TO RIGHT: Filtered through the gossamer linen window treatments, the light in the bedroom becomes dreamlike. A few carefully curated items punctuate the space. Soft geometries are woven into the gold-and-pearl-hued wool-and-silk rug. An effulgent parcel-gilt detail of the lacquered chinoiserie cabinet.

ABOVE AND OPPOSITE: The primary bath is cleansed of visual noise. The dove-gray veining of the statuary marble floor and the muted, sheer curtains help blur the lines between soft and hard surfaces. FOLLOWING PAGES: Elevated amidst the trees, the office is a tranquil aerie for our client. Suspended from the vaulted ceiling is a polygonal lantern that echoes the angular shape of the room.

OPPOSITE: The homeowner fell in love with Janaina Tschäpe's etching *Untitled* (2023) at Art Basel, and it now brings dynamic presence to the family gathering space.

ABOVE, LEFT TO RIGHT: The second office is home to an architectural trestle desk in solid wenge with a glass-and-leather top. Built-in shelving shelters favorite objects and books. We designed a custom base for a stoneware vessel so it would be perfectly framed by the portal in the staircase wall. The clients are dedicated oenophiles; we created a transportive candle-lit tasting room with a banquette and small oak tables.

ABOVE AND OPPOSITE: We had the privilege of curating all of the decorative and functional accessories for the home to ensure well-appointed spaces from table to bath. Here, the terrace is set for dinner al fresco.

OPPOSITE: An arched gateway leads to the pool lawn. ABOVE: Welcoming McKinnon and Harris dining tables are sheltered by trident maples.

Outside of Time

A road can feel like a secret in Lowcountry. Curving beneath canopies of ancient oak draped in Spanish moss and resurrection fern, this sand-paved drive is a hushed transition to our home. To the east, a pond flows in tides of water and light. To the west, a salt marsh is habitat to deer, alligator, and pink spoonbills on their vast wings. Our house sits amidst this green world. It's a refuge that exists outside of time.

Architect James Choate designed the residence to commingle with the land: a series of pavilions of wood, stone, and glass, one wing has already been reclaimed by nature, enveloped by creeping fig. My husband originally built the home with his son, and he later extended it, adding a primary bedroom suite. We also updated its surfaces, replacing sheetrock with an organic material palette of wenge, cedar, and white oak.

The heart of the house is the long room, a space 50 feet in length where 22-foot-high ceilings ascend in tiers of wood, board-formed concrete, and blackened steel. The full-height windows offer views of the surrounding landscape and of the live oaks reaching from ground to sky. This space is a vitrine writ large for the beloved art, antiques, and objects we've collected on our travels: works by artists and friends, Japanese ceramics and ikebana baskets, vintage pieces discovered at Les Puces in Paris. Most recently, at Axel Vervoordt's Antwerp gallery, Kanaal, we acquired two vessels by contemporary ceramicist Shiro Tsujimura. His layered glazed pieces are of the earth, and have such wabi-sabi beauty that they feel at home here.

PAGE 46: A tidal creek flows through the salt marsh to the pond. PREVIOUS PAGES: The architecture of the home is an elemental composition of raw wood, blackened steel, and poured concrete. OPPOSITE: The stone fireplace was laid by hand. Stonemasons have personal signatures, so to achieve perfectly imperfect stacking, we rotated the masons to ensure a unique composition. Board-formed concrete flanks the hearth.

RIGHT: The long room, with its open plan, offers breathing space and allows us to entertain with ease. PAGE 54: A still life includes a wooden bowl by British artist Joel Parkes. PAGE 55: Against the back wall is an antique sculptor's stand topped with a Chinese earthenware pot. The standing lamp is Liaigre.

ABOVE, LEFT TO RIGHT: In the library, a vintage Japanese ikebana basket, one of a collection I acquired from a friend, nestles amidst books. An antique Italian oak table set with a pair of circa-1920s French milk-glass lamps serves as a bar and is stocked with vintage silver barware found at Les Puces. A dried *Cecropia* leaf rests in an ebonized bowl. The library sitting area is home to an elegant mahogany side table from my husband's collection of American Federal furniture.

PAGE 58: The foyer is a vertical intersection of wood, stone, steel, and concrete. PAGE 59: The library was my husband's study (he commissioned the desk) until I commandeered it. *Black Torrington #6* (2019), a haunting work by Kate Hunt, hangs above the fireplace. RIGHT: In our intimate dining room hang two paintings of nearby fields, commissioned from American landscape artist Michael Dines. The director's chairs are Liaigre. The glassware is vintage French bistro.

Functionally, the house needed to work for my husband and myself, as well as for extended family gatherings. We're very fortunate to have several of our children nearby, and the house is alive with activity year-round. In the long room, I designed smaller furniture groupings within this large volume to create warmth and intimacy. In the morning, I'm often here on a sofa with our dog, Biscuit, as the light is so dappled and soft. In the evening, we are cocooned in the paneled library, its floor-to-ceiling window treatments enveloping us.

In the primary bedroom layers of custom bed-hangings and linen curtains filter the eastern light, and the scrim flickers with bird shadow and swaying moss. Our loft guestroom has an aerial view of the live oaks, and when we aren't hosting guests, my husband and I will often retreat to its private covered terrace for breakfast or dinner. It also offers a very dramatic vista when the storms roll in.

In a glass house, you are a witness to nature, and are witnessed by it. We frequently have a family of raccoons who on occasion press their faces to the glass to watch us! Each season brings a different beauty: in the winter, hundreds of egrets nest in trees beneath the moon. Spring is an effulgence of green. In summer, we are watchful as our local alligators sun themselves on our dike. And on autumn evenings, in perfect driving weather, we take to the road in the vintage Defender, ready to discover new secrets.

OPPOSITE: For me, creating tablescapes is a source of joy. The tablecloth is by Peter Dunham. The Match pewter is handmade in Italy, and the glass platter is Tiffany. The petite salt dishes were handmade by the sister of a friend.

RIGHT: The arboreal kitchen is a nest of wenge and white oak, with the cabinetry finished with stain and limewash. The graphite drawings were purchased on a trip to Havana.

ABOVE: The primary bedroom is a palimpsest of honeyed tones—diaphanous layers of custom bed drapery and linen curtain panels filter the eastern light. Diffusing the light from the pond, the scrims flicker with shadows of birds and swaying moss. The Phillip Jeffries woven wallcovering further softens and layers the room. OPPOSITE: A midcentury modern lamp and a photograph by Rena Bass Forman.

ABOVE, LEFT TO RIGHT: The yin and yang of Calacatta marble and wenge give the primary bath strength and serenity. The tub is Victoria + Albert. A vignette of sea sponge, shells, and driftwood. The guest bath overlooks the marsh and is supremely tranquil; bathing here is like bathing en plein air.

ABOVE: We've carved out and cultivated a little flower and herb garden. Just standing and breathing in the earthy, sensual fragrance is restorative.
OPPOSITE: Entertaining our family and friends, especially outdoors, is one of the great joys of my life. The landscape is a sublime setting, and we're often graced by visits from deer and foxes.

Coastal Light

You wake to the sound of waves, to the feel of air warmed by sun. Looking out the bedroom window, you visually swim in the Gulf of Mexico. "To be dissolved into something complete and great" is how Willa Cather described happiness; to be absorbed like salt into the sea. In this beachfront home, we sought to summon that feeling at all vantage points. Together with Atlanta architect T. S. Adams, we envisioned a home that would engender the stillness and wholeness that occur when all the senses are connected to nature.

Our clients had acquired one of the only remaining oceanfront properties along the coastline of 30A in Seaside, Florida. Designed by architects and urban planners Andrés Duany and Elizabeth Plater-Zyberk, Seaside is considered the first New Urbanist community (the team would go on to design Alys Beach). It is iconic both as a thriving community built on the principles of walkability and indoor/outdoor living and as the site of residences designed by renowned architects, including Robert A. M. Stern, Steven Holl, and Deborah Berke.

This spectacular commission would be the vacation home for a family from the Atlanta area who had been visiting Seaside for many years. The four-story wooden structure soars up from the very edge of the land as if mainsail set.

PAGE 72: With its sweeping staircase and striking chocolate-and-white marble mosaic floor, the foyer makes a dramatic first impression. PAGE 74: The graceful arched passageway from foyer to living room. PAGE 75: Stepping over the threshold, guests are met by a statement-making Susan Hable work on paper in the entry foyer. OPPOSITE: A breathtaking vista of the Gulf of Mexico commands the great room. The elevated siting of the house enables spectacular vantage points—unobstructed views of crystal-clear water and white sand.

RIGHT: Architectural symmetry defines the living room, from the coffered ceiling to the pair of ox-eye windows. FOLLOWING PAGES: Cast stone, cerused oak, and fringed linen add organic elements to the living room's refined structure.

ABOVE, LEFT TO RIGHT: In the foyer powder room, the antiqued mirror reflects a rare Avalanche dolomite marble whose veining evokes the nearby waves. A single stem in a Japanese bronze vase. In the dining area, the window wall opens onto the pool; woven leather-and-bamboo chairs create a casual, communal gathering place. The richness of the tabletop composition is evocative of a still life.

That loftiness carries inside, taking shape in walls and ceilings, marble and tile, and furnishings and fabrics washed in white. The clarity of color is dazzling in the clear coastal light and frames the ever-shifting blues of horizon and ocean.

Dressing the rooms are refined natural textures, ever-present from first to fourth story. After entering the house through the arched front gates and sun-filled breezeway, in the great room you'll find club chairs with a wonderful fringed fabric that evokes deckled-edge paper, and a console with rough-hewn, cast-stone legs. In the primary bedroom, we chose the subtlest of textures: seating in matelassé cotton, embroidered window treatments, and side tables in shagreen—an organic yet sophisticated material palette, gentle to the touch.

This serene lightness of color and texture is a reminder of all the immaterial things that give us peace—the ocean air wafting over us at night, the sound of gulls in the morning, and the feeling of weightlessness when submerged in the sea.

OPPOSITE: Two of my favorite moments in the kitchen are the louvered pantry doors and the half-door, created for the family's beloved dogs. The space is a play of plaster, limestone, and marble, and though the overall palette appears monochromatic, there are myriad variations on white. Finishes—matte for the plaster, high gloss for the trim, the gleam of nickel—add further dimension.

ABOVE: The art of tabletop is an intrinsic part of my practice, and a personal passion. I'm also privileged to work with phenomenally talented stylists. This setting is all about sensuality of shape: the spherical, apothecary-style vase; the looping arms of the ceramic bowl; the organic form of a pot holding white peonies.
OPPOSITE: At the client's request, we incorporated pattern in the window treatments, but purposefully kept them color-neutral so they would not compete with the view. The embroidery adds further dimension.

The bleached hues of the primary bedroom make it float amidst the sweeping, 180-degree views of the Gulf of Mexico; the windows open to the sound of the surf.

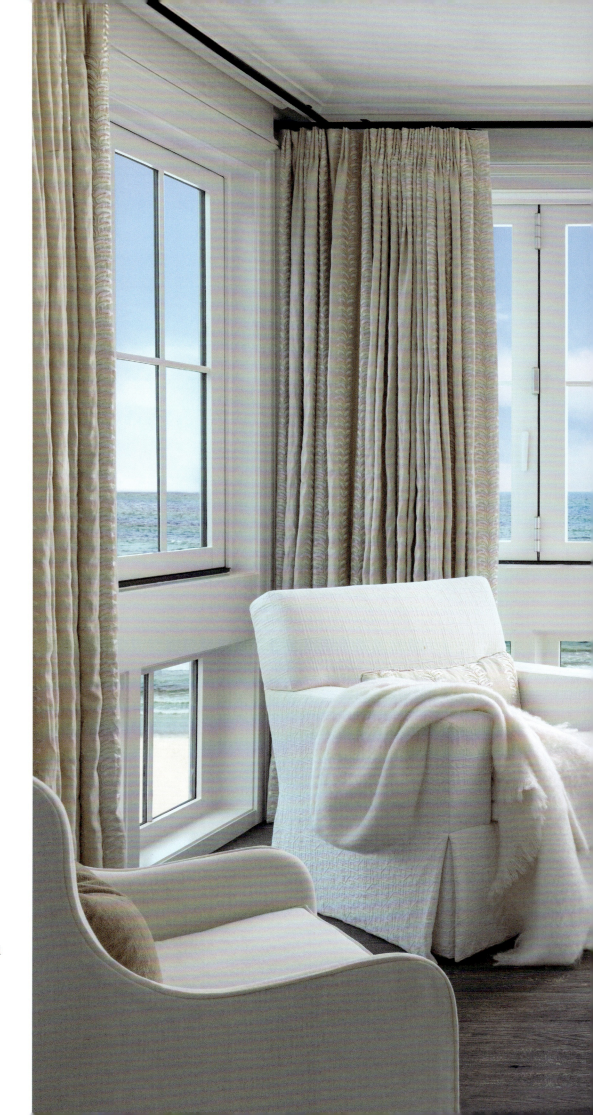

In the primary bedroom suite, husband and wife each have their own bath and wardrobe; the window bay, however, was specifically designed for two.

A Grounded Spirit

Ideally a home reflects the soul of the person who lives within it. This house is privileged to have an owner whose kindness and warmth of spirit infuse its rooms. William Hazlitt, the great nineteenth-century philosopher of the aesthetic, wrote, "Grace has been defined as the outward expression of the inward harmony of the soul." It was our good fortune to translate this client's inner beauty into her surroundings.

Situated on the edge of a lake, with only water and woods in view, this residence has the feel of a modern villa. Designed by architect Jeffrey Dungan, the stone and terracotta tile buildings enclose an entry courtyard, while the lake-facing grounds unfold in lush lawns and groves. Here, one is always connected to place—whether meditating in the garden or stepping onto a terrace to find a moment of stillness, one breathes the deep green of the landscape.

The home is beautifully sited and beautifully crafted. Devoted to fine materials and detail, Jeff was exacting down to the interior finishes. Throughout the home, timber beams, rough-hewn stone, and wood-paneled rooms provided a rich canvas upon which to layer textures that reflected the client's energetic embrace. Even the kitchen, with its soft, cerused-wood ceiling and muted palette made luminous by a skylight, is serene.

PAGE 92: The study has such a painterly atmosphere; it is always bathed in a Vermeer light. The room is paneled in a beautiful honey-toned oak and designed to be simple, almost monastic—just a desk and chair, and a window seat in the alcove. OPPOSITE: With its vaulted and beamed ceiling, the dining space offered an opportunity to let the architecture sing. Focus is trained on the richness of the wood, stone, and plaster.

ABOVE: In the calm, inviting living room, an enchanting petite window is one of the architect's signature moments. OPPOSITE: In the same room, lounge chairs are gathered in a classic configuration around the hearth.

ABOVE, LEFT TO RIGHT: The Italianate stone exterior with brick detail at the windows. In the primary bedroom, the lounge chair and ottoman are upholstered in an antique linen velvet, creating the perfect place to curl up with a cashmere throw and a book; three grisaille Italian villa custom decorative panels by de Gournay set the scene. An antique glass-paneled door leads from the kitchen into her office. In the primary bedroom, the fireplace is sited in the corner of the room so as not to block the view of the lake.

This is a traditional home with a European sense of ease—though it is sophisticated and tailored, the atmosphere is relaxed. We paired classic contemporary pieces with antiques and custom elements; one of my favorite vignettes comprises a sumptuous lounge chair and a petite drinks table set against a custom de Gournay triptych of a classical villa. Each room has a moment of refuge like this for body and mind—the study window seat with pillows sheathed in velvet, the primary bedroom with headboard wrapped in cashmere. We also appointed these spaces with finishing touches—armfuls of flowers from the garden, bed linens stitched with custom embroidery, an octet of luminous Neapolitan oil paintings—to stir the senses.

When someone is genuinely warm and authentically gracious, like our client, those qualities emanate from within. There is an inner glow that comes from a grounded spirit. In an ideal setting, a home mirrors this radiance: its artwork inspires, its antiques create connection across time, the comfort and beauty of its rooms bring peace. It is a symbiotic relationship, creating the soul of a home.

OPPOSITE: In the warmth of the kitchen keeping room, a mohair-covered chair invites lounging in front of the fire. The flow of the rooms can be seen from this vantage point—the enfilade of keeping room, dining room, and living room.

RIGHT: Natural light floods the formal dining room where the family gathers. The dining room, adjacent to the kitchen yet separated from it, allows a glimpse into the breakfast nook, while the fireplace screens the kitchen working space.
FOLLOWING PAGES: The kitchen has a rustic yet refined ambience with its vaulted, limewashed oak ceiling and antique beams, all framed by a stone arch.

ABOVE, LEFT TO RIGHT: A set of six intaglios grace the stairs leading up from the foyer. The elegant bar opposite the study is a spot for a civilized cocktail and represents masterful use of an alcove. A sculptural stone detail of the mantelpiece in the downstairs family room, a space with serenity and style.

ABOVE: The primary bedroom is a study in oyster and pearl hues. OPPOSITE: The romantic branching-iron canopy bed features a headboard in white cashmere, above which hangs a beautifully patinated seventeenth-century Spanish carved-wood relief.

A Dream the Sea Makes

Contoured by the tides and lit by the southeastern sun, the sea islands of the Georgia coast are breathtakingly beautiful. An island, wrote poet A. R. Ammons, is "a dream the sea makes." In the case of Sea Island, it was formed in tandem with a visionary developer. Founded nearly a century ago by an automobile magnate and his family, Sea Island is a private resort community. It is home to the legendary Cloister, a 1928 Spanish Revival-style hotel designed by Addison Mizner, who introduced the Mediterranean vernacular to Palm Beach and the region.

I've been designing homes on Sea Island since my children were young, and visiting for even longer. So, I was delighted when a wonderful couple commissioned us for the interiors of this new residence. Envisioned as a getaway where they could rest, restore, and entertain family, the home exudes the gracious hospitality for which Sea Island is so beloved.

PAGE 110 AND OPPOSITE: With its sculptural floating stair and floor-to-ceiling windows, the foyer is a breathtaking space to welcome guests.

Tucked into a lush landscape, this home was tailored to indoor/outdoor living, from the soaring window walls to the poolside dining areas. To enhance the connection to site by drawing on the organic textures of the live oaks and salt grass, we wove layers of natural materials—wood, wicker, jute—throughout. Subtle botanical motifs bloom on fabrics, and local birds take migratory paths in prints and photographs. We designed not only indoor spaces, but a screened porch, where one can enjoy lunch at the table or while away the afternoon in a lounge chair with sweet tea and a book.

This residence has the easy elegance of an island home. In the stunning all-white foyer, the curved staircase with its slender black rails is refined in its simplicity. Moving into the living room, one is elevated by the palette of diaphanous tones. It is also the perfect place to welcome friends for pre-dinner cocktails, preferably at the golden hour.

OPPOSITE: An egret journeys through the Sea Island light and air in Kate Griswold's photograph. The room takes on a wonderful pale, bleached-out tonality when washed in sun.

ABOVE, LEFT TO RIGHT: A view from the living room to the pool. In the foyer, an antique elm sculptor's stand supports a ceramic urn, lending soul and presence to the space. In the breakfast room, wicker chairs with sensual silhouettes resemble ladies in skirts. The kitchen is a perfect place for relaxed family dining.

OPPOSITE AND ABOVE: The primary bedroom wraps those who enter it in the warmth of caramel colors and natural textures. The cording of the bedposts is finely woven lampakanay rope. The bench is dressed in a delicate, embroidered abstract paisley.

ABOVE: We curate objects very intentionally—in the primary suite, a vintage canvas-and-leather safari chair, and in the primary bath, a wonderfully quirky antique stool (pictured opposite) add patina to these newly built spaces.
OPPOSITE: The primary bath features shades of white to soothing effect.

PREVIOUS PAGES: The screened porch beckons. This is the space where everyone gathers each day, in the cool of the morning or in the evening to sit with glasses of wine. ABOVE AND OPPOSITE: A pair of vintage cast-stone French urns sit atop the rough-hewn double console table that separates the dining and sitting areas.

Solidity and Strength

Mountain time is deep time, measured in epochs of geological formation. Encountering the Grand Teton range in Wyoming, one is oriented in this dimension—its stillness and vastness transcend conventional time. This sense of the long view was the foundation for this Jackson Hole residence; built to endure, it was planned from the start as a home for the clients' children, grandchildren, and generations to come. My relationship with the clients is also a long-term one. We met seventeen years ago when I designed their home in Atlanta, when we and they had small children. The clients had a vacation house in Jackson Hole for many years, but when this site in a sublime valley became available, they decided to build their legacy.

We worked with the architects from conception to completion of interior finishes and spaces. Peaked and vaulted rooms took shape in stone, rough-hewn wood–beams, and steel-frame windows—all reminders of the elemental topography of the site. Our material language was likewise organic yet clean: natural stone slabs of Jurassic gray granite, limestone flooring, fabrics in alpaca and antique Japanese hemp. We edged the warmly modernist spaces with black. Black has the sharpness of fractured flint, and we used it to add graphic power, lining doorways with blackened, waxed-steel casings, utilizing graphite granite countertops in the kitchen, and designing an expansive shou sugi ban bar.

PAGE 126: *Helene* by Sabine Maes (2021) anchors the living room and is a powerful focal point in a graphic palette of black and white. OPPOSITE: In the foyer, the groin-vaulted ceiling and slurried fieldstone walls form an almost monastic envelope for art and objects.

ABOVE: Steel windows frame the expansive views. OPPOSITE: The spectacular three peaks of the Grand Tetons are echoed by the vaulted living room in just one of this home's many opportunities to marvel at the awe-inspiring surroundings. FOLLOWING PAGES: The library epitomizes the home's refined mountain aesthetic: it is nature-inspired but has a modern sensibility. We placed a leather-topped table amidst the wood beams and stone. Our client's collection of Native American basketry is seen here and throughout the house.

ABOVE, LEFT TO RIGHT: An arch lined with blackened steel connects the study to the living room. An antique Scottish chair sits by the kitchen hearth. We juxtaposed the Jurassic gray granite countertop with sleek drawer pulls. To the right of the front door, an arched doorway leads into this dreamy, incredible space.

OPPOSITE: The spectacular antique English table, rustic Italian pine armoire, and Belgian coffer are all from iconic antique dealer Randall Tysinger. ABOVE: Dining room artwork is by Kader Boly. FOLLOWING PAGES: This is a home destined for entertaining, and the open kitchen enables an easy flow of family and guests. It tells a story of materiality—the plaster pendants, the shou sugi ban base of the island topped with Jurassic gray granite, the hand-hewn beams. Though many types of wood are juxtaposed, they rest together beautifully.

PREVIOUS PAGES: In the kitchen keeping room, steel floor-to-ceiling windows frame a picturesque landscape that was designed for the site. The pond and grasses are also a wonderful natural habitat—elk and moose meander through day and night. The clients are in this sitting room every single morning with coffee, and at night with scotch. The barrel chairs—upholstered in a charcoal-hued wool—embrace you. OPPOSITE: The mudroom is where the ski equipment and snowboards live. ABOVE: Down the hall is an elegant but very functional back pantry—it is a space where guests can meet in the morning for hot chocolate or sip wine après ski.

The clients were completely engaged in the entire design process and appreciated the stories behind artisanal techniques. Throughout the course of the project, we sourced together internationally and locally, from Antwerp to Jackson Hole, for antiques, artifacts, and contemporary craft. Among the many finds—a fabulous antique Scottish chair, a hand-carved ebonized stool by contemporary woodworker Caleb Woodard, and gorgeous vintage Moroccan rugs.

A massing of peaks and planes, the home stretches out with solidity and strength. When one sits fireside at the rear of the property, in the shadow of the ancient form of the Tetons, mountains of the land become mountains of the mind. Cloaked in snow and stars and infinite years, the same peaks will be viewed from this home for generations.

OPPOSITE: There are two guest suites in the home on the main level. In one, we incorporated the daybed with the clients' grandchildren in mind, as well as to give guests a place to slip away for a quiet moment.

ABOVE, LEFT TO RIGHT: In one guestroom, luscious alpaca window treatments can be drawn to sleep late. The view in the primary bedroom from the bed to the pond. In another guestroom, curling up among rustic linens is a delicious retreat on cool evenings. The vintage leather gym bench adds patina and personality.

ABOVE: In the summer, visitors explore the landscape on a hike or a ride, then return to a home that is one with the land. Outdoor dining is an important part of that experience. OPPOSITE: With this view, dining al fresco is a regular ritual. FOLLOWING PAGES: In winter the property can be covered by five feet of snow, but in summer the aspen leaves shimmer and the tall grass moves in the breeze. It is magical.

A Study in Clarity

A villa composed of geometries in white, this home is a study in clarity. Designed by architect Jeffrey Dungan, this residence at Alys Beach—an iconic New Urbanist community—is a contemporary gothic beach house. Near the shore of the Gulf of Mexico, it sings with pointed arches and windows, lyrical vaulted ceilings, and a central courtyard, as well as an astonishing 40-foot tower.

All structures at Alys Beach are a mandated, signature, dazzling white, but at this residence pristineness was softened by Jeff's interior surfaces: artisanal zellige tile, board-formed concrete, shou sugi ban planking, and spidery black-veined marble. Stepping into these breathtaking spaces, we knew the furnishings needed to have the same sculptural presence. We approached the interiors judiciously, selecting pieces with strength of form and material richness.

For the great room, with its soaring wall of board-formed concrete, we composed a grouping of antique and vintage pieces: a nineteenth-century French stool, a 1960s Turkish kilim, a tribal Nagaland chair with beautiful graining, a custom Italian marble coffee table, and a diminutive wood-and-

PAGE 153: In the great room, two abstract works echo the painterly quality of the board-formed concrete. PAGES 154 AND 155: Intending to be minimalist, the architect channeled Carlo Scarpa in creating the spare volume of the great room; we followed suit by giving the artful furnishings room to breathe. OPPOSITE: A view into the kitchen from the great room; carefully selected wooden and woven pieces in organic shapes imbue the space with a wabi-sabi sensibility.

RIGHT: The kitchen glimpsed through the chamfered arch opening. The custom cabinetry, masterfully crafted in reeded glass and aged brass, displays white ceramics.
PAGES 160 AND 161: The sleek, shadowy material palette is a sophisticated backdrop for entertaining.

leather African chair. The strength of their shapes enables them to hold their own in this expansive space. For the office, entirely and sublimely clad by Jeff in ink-black shou sugi ban, we chose an ebonized writing desk, a wood-and-leather director's chair, and a curvaceous pair of vintage 1960s Danish armchairs. In the primary bedroom, with its poetic vaulted ceiling and monastic beauty, we walked softly, allowing the space to be spare and contemplative.

I wanted this home to have the atmosphere of a spiritual space, and that feeling intensifies on the second-floor terrace. It is breathtaking—an oasis Jeff conjured of marble, water, air, and sun. What to add except a few minimalist pieces on which to sit and drink it all in?

PREVIOUS PAGES: The textural elements of the office—a charcoal cerused-oak writing desk and glossy black cabinet against a backdrop of deep black shou sugi ban—create an enveloping refuge. OPPOSITE: In the primary bedroom, groin vaulting evokes a monk's cell; the space is infused with atmospheric light yet grounded by the boldness of the Turkish kilim.

ABOVE, LEFT TO RIGHT: High-contrast studies: In the primary suite bath, shower doors in reeded glass and aged brass frame the spectacular black-and-white Quebec quartzite. The same stone is incorporated into the statement-making vanity. In the guest suite, an ebony-hued shower with handmade Moroccan zellige tiles creates a dramatic moment. The stunning black veining in the quartzite is equally eye-catching.

A Storybook Made Real

PREVIOUS PAGES: The convergence of pecky cypress paneling, limewashed beams, and Belgian bluestone is a material tour-de-force in the entry hall. ABOVE: Entry to the main foyer is through a charming, cottage-like front door. OPPOSITE: At the end of the two-tiered foyer, the refined grouping of Louis XVI chairs at a Rose Tarlow table invites a moment of pause.

There are places that offer the enchantment of intimacy, while others cast the spell of the expansive. At this storybook home on Kiawah Island, one experiences both. Unfolding in gabled roofs and arched doorways, this residence rises from the landscape with the Voysey-esque charm of an English country seat. Elevated high on the dunes, it is also *face en face* with the horizon, in dialogue with the clouds and the infinite blue. It's a gift to stand in such sublime surroundings.

This is a deeply layered home. From siting to finishes, it was crafted by architect D. Stanley Dixon to endure. Our interior design is rooted in his architectural vision. Stan and I have worked together on several homes, and collaborating with him on this project was an exceptional joy. Here, he adapted traditional English architecture to sing with the landscape and light of the South Carolina coast. For example, while elements of the design trace back to British Arts and Crafts, he chose to finish the exterior of the home in tabby, a regional material incorporating crushed oyster shells. He meticulously matched the color to the taupe-gray beaches that are characteristic of the island.

OPPOSITE: In the passage between the kitchen entry and the main stair hall, the play of light on Venetian plaster speaks to the superb level of finish.

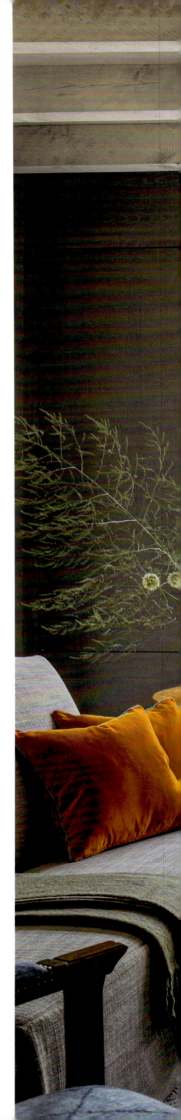

RIGHT: The handsome library in the front of the house acts as the winter room. From here, the view is of the verdant landscape in the front of the house.
PAGE 176: An antique chest and mirror create a storied moment. PAGE 177: A sublime corner is perfect for settling in with a favorite book.

Inside, he established a material envelope of pecky cypress, cerused oak, English Yorkstone, and limewashed white oak that feels both rustic and refined. We responded to that with a textural language of layered linen, block-print cottons, and touches of cashmere and alpaca. Together they create a quiet elegance that transcends the seasons. In the enfilade of light-washed front rooms, family and friends sink into linen-covered armchairs, curl up on the wicker sofa by the hearth, or gather in the formal dining room, luminous in silvery Venetian plaster.

This is also a marvelous place for entertaining. When designing spaces, I'm motivated by the pursuit of happiness, and this is a space for living well. Summer is high season for family gathering, and events often center around the pool in its spectacular setting, with children splashing while recumbent adults soak in the warmth and the coastal breeze. And when guests are ready to retire, they head to the pool house, an intimately scaled space that provides additional accommodation. There they can climb into the snug daybed and sleep under the eaves.

In English fairy tales, a path often meanders over the moors and crofts, and here, a dreamlike boardwalk rises and falls over the dunes. Bridging shelter and nature, it is a passage that feels almost mythic, ultimately delivering you to the edge of the sea.

OPPOSITE: An elevated ambience and enveloping, high-back armchairs encourage guests to linger in the formal dining room.

ABOVE: The round table and chairs anchor a raised entry that sits between the living and dining rooms. OPPOSITE: Club chairs are perches for taking in the vast horizons.

PREVIOUS PAGES: The variations in handmade tiles add interest to the backsplash. ABOVE, LEFT TO RIGHT: One of the kitchen's signature oculus windows, set within the pure expanse of white tiles. A beautiful summer harvest rests on the countertop. Coastal light illuminates the pantry. Nailhead detailing on the counter stools. PAGE 186: In the kitchen keeping room, a painted cabinet provides artful alcoves for books, florals, and *objets*. PAGE 187: The keeping room features several distinct seating areas, from club chairs for lounging to a breakfast table for family dining.

The pale palette of the primary bedroom is so restful that one cannot help but recline on the chaise and take in sweeping vistas of the Atlantic.

ABOVE: The primary bedroom transitions to a sitting room and her office. OPPOSITE: The office is a perfect place to retreat midday for a quiet moment. De Le Cuona fabric wraps the sofa.

Soaking in the landscape and light in the primary bath. FOLLOWING PAGES: French doors, framed by luxurious window treatments, lead to a terrace off a bedroom—a heavenly place to while away the morning hours.

ABOVE: A stairway in the pool house to the guest quarters above.
OPPOSITE: In the laundry room, all utilitarian elements
are concealed, enabling it to do double duty as a cutting room.

ABOVE AND OPPOSITE: The inviting screened porch beckons for brunch or lingering in front of the hearth at sundown. FOLLOWING PAGES: The storybook exterior.

Creativity in Dialogue

In the main stair hall, its plasterwork honed by light, a terracotta figure presides over an entry. Its presence stirs the atmosphere like a votive. Sculpted by twentieth-century artist Henry Kreis, this figure of a mother and child establishes the artistic lineage of one of the owners of this newly built residence: the home was commissioned by Kreis's granddaughter and her husband. The couple wanted a residence to house both their family and its inherited collection of art and called upon architect Peter Block. Peter is renowned for translating traditional and European disciplines into contemporary structures; his sense of materiality and history was a perfect fit for the clients' affinity for Belgian design. This was a dream project that also allowed us to immerse ourselves in the Flemish aesthetic, about which we're both passionate.

Belgian interiors have long been a touchpoint for me. In their atmospheric spaces, the invisible is as important as the visible. A space's energy and presence must move and inspire as much as what's placed within it. In this home, we worked to achieve that with gestures of light. Peter's vision ensured that each room had at least two windows, and we choreographed in chiaroscuro: a chapel-like white bedroom segues into a deep gray sitting room. A bright kitchen meets an iron-hued pantry. Shadows come to rest in an alcove. We were inspired, as well, by the Flemish veneration of natural materials. Peter's palette—wire-brushed European oak, limewashed brick, Marmorino plaster—is high touch. We extended that sensuality into the interiors. The feeling against the skin of glazed earthenware, of the worn oak of a farm table, of soft, fine European linen brings soulfulness to the experience of home.

PAGE 202: Equestrian maquettes by our client's grandfather, the late sculptor Henry Kreis, stand foursquare on shelves in the living room. PAGE 204: The graceful entranceway passage. PAGE 205: In the foyer, two liturgical works by the artist hover in shadow and light. OPPOSITE: Composing a still life is another source of joy for me—here, an antique elm altar table is set with Japanese candlesticks and a double-spout vessel. A French cast-iron fire log foundry rests beneath.

I had the privilege of placing the family's archival collection in these artful rooms. Sculptor Henry Kreis is known for his elegant, classically inspired work. In the 1920s, he studied at the Beaux-Arts Institute of Design in New York. He then went on to assist the artist Paul Manship, creator of the monumental Prometheus at Rockefeller Center. Kreis's pieces are in many collections, including the permanent collection of the Whitney Museum of American Art. Our client had inherited some of her grandfather's work, and together we lovingly curated and installed the pieces throughout the home. We found pedestals for Kreis's large-scale figures, and placed noble little equines in dialogue with earthenware vessels. We ensconced tiny formal maquettes on shelves and framed his award-winning numismatic work. One afternoon the client came to me with another treasure: a canvas roll containing her grandfather's sculpting tools. We shadowboxed these precious artifacts, and they now overlook the family room.

And there was another formative artist in the family: Patricia Alden Kreis, a printmaker, was Henry Kreis's wife and the client's grandmother. It was an inspiration to curate and frame her work as well; we made a grouping of nine silkscreen prints the dining room's focal point. I love that the pair's creativity is now in dialogue, its presence felt throughout the house—the interweaving of art and family made visible.

PREVIOUS PAGES: The stunning living room has a Belgian sensibility with cool grays; the edited space frames the lyrical natural and built elements. OPPOSITE: Nine works by the client's grandmother, also an artist and printmaker, grace the dining room.

PAGE 212: A photograph by Kreis of one of his superb figurative works. PAGE 213: In the keeping room, an intimate corner in front of the hearth provides a canvas for a black-and-white vignette; the shelves display selections of Kreis's numismatic work. OPPOSITE: We framed the artist's sculpting tools and medals to bring his presence to the family room.

PREVIOUS PAGES: The stunning black-and-white kitchen continues the high-contrast palette of the keeping room. ABOVE: Black iron and antique mirror cabinetry add a graphic touch. OPPOSITE: The deep gray hue in the butler's pantry adds nuance to the color story. FOLLOWING PAGES: In the breakfast room, one can commune with the trees. The paneled walls add a layer of rich rusticity, melding the room with the woods beyond.

ABOVE, LEFT TO RIGHT: A dusky landscape by Michael Dines floats in the keeping room. A collection of clay maquettes by Kreis; the centerpiece is a vintage cover of *Fortune* magazine featuring his work. The dark and moody sitting room, with its high-gloss lacquered walls, reflects light cast through the linen scrim. The pristine white bath features floor-to-ceiling windows that look out upon the lawn. FOLLOWING PAGES: The screen porch holds the outdoor dining area, highly textural in rough-sawn wood and slurried brick.

Elegance and Repose

This place of elegant repose has the settled quality of a home that has held families for a century. A 1920s dwelling in Buckhead, not far from my own home in Atlanta, this residence has captured my heart. I've had the privilege of designing this very special house three times, for three different owners. I have known it past and present, and most recently I designed it to welcome the coming generation.

Returning to this elegant property was like seeing a very dear old friend. I wandered the rooms, reconnecting with the intimate scale, the gorgeous light. To honor this grand dame and create the traditional look the clients sought, my team and I would speak to its classicism and sense of place. However, anticipating that the home would be full of the clients' children and grandchildren, we didn't want it to be exceedingly formal.

We envisioned spaces that were refined, but not imposing. Tailored but plush sofas; generous, upholstered dining chairs; and a tufted ottoman perfect for backgammon or storytime all invite gathering—and lingering. With their soft lamplight and antique rugs, these rooms have an aura of timelessness.

PAGE 226: In the primary bedroom, a chinoiserie secretary that was discovered by the client at the Palm Beach Show. A bergère chair reupholstered in a rich, luminous Loro Piana embroidered fabric establishes the blue leitmotif that runs throughout the home.
PREVIOUS PAGES: The salon is historically layered from the ground up, its foundation an antique Mahal rug, upon which sit a nineteenth-century Italian burl walnut commode and a nineteenth-century mahogany English architect's table (which now enjoys life as a game table). OPPOSITE: The salon view of the gracious first-floor enfilade.

Throughout the course of the project, the clients cultivated their growing interest in nineteenth- and early twentieth-century American and European art, and we collected an array of antique furnishings and objets d'art. The clients are particularly fond of French decorative arts, and we selected wonderful antique pieces to grace each room.

The grounds feel equally continental. The original landscape architect, Jeremy Spearman, returned to cultivate and reinvigorate the dreamy lawns and gardens. At the rear of the house, deep green climbing vines drape over the pierced brick wall, and a floriated path rings a circular garden. In front, glorious mature trees shelter the approach, leaving only the need for the simplicity of a lawn and hedges.

Redesigning a home I've previously decorated is an intimate form of time travel. I can feel the shifts in atmosphere and energy that have occurred in the intervening years. Every space has an identity. This one feels so very kindred to my own.

OPPOSITE: In the dining room, a Willard Metcalf winter landscape of snow and wide blue sky inhabits the space above the eighteenth-century Lyonnaise Régence commode.

ABOVE, LEFT TO RIGHT: One of a pair of antique hand-painted English armchairs reupholstered in celadon-blue Loro Piana fabric. A detail of the circa 1670 mirror that hangs above the hearth, discovered in Antwerp at Axel Vervoordt. A wisp of blue cashmere in the salon, and a child's chair—a sweet and welcoming gesture for the grandchildren. In addition to being rich in decorative history, the salon has been the setting for many family memories.

ABOVE AND OPPOSITE: The welcoming study invites ensconcing oneself on the sofa—legs resting on the tufted ottoman—and watching life unfold. The grasscloth wallcovering and antique Oushak rug make the space all the more enveloping.

PAGE 238: In the foyer, we juxtaposed this whimsical nineteenth-century French demilune, one of a pair, with the stately front door. PAGE 239: In his office, an antique French farm table is a workspace with age and soul. A night scene by William Glackens emanates magic into the room. OPPOSITE: In her office, atop the desk is a pair of figurative nineteenth-century bronze-and-marble lamps, while below is a hand-carved walnut Georgian marchepied. ABOVE: In the powder room, the block print wallcovering extends the floral motif of the antique Venetian mirror.

ABOVE: The butler's pantry is a warm and sunlit spot. The sapphire-blue floral Roman shade teeming with flora and fauna injects jewel-like color into the otherwise muted space. OPPOSITE: In the breakfast room, the pattern from the window treatment carries onto the seat cushions of the Gustavian chairs.

PREVIOUS PAGES: The primary bedroom is sumptuously appointed and interlaced with bold moments, such as the swooping curves of the Venetian, iron canopy bed and the luxuriant, deeply folded drapery. ABOVE, LEFT TO RIGHT: The crackled lacquer chinoiserie bed table serves as both bookstand and tray for leisurely mornings. Floriated linen trims the drapery. Alabaster candle-lamps rest on a hand-painted Swedish chest. A painterly scene in hazy blue that fills my soul—a circa 1920 bergère and ottoman atop an antique Tabriz rug.

ABOVE AND OPPOSITE: Fresh dahlias and crisp Italian linens are gracious gestures in a guest bedroom. The chest is a circa 1890 French washstand.
FOLLOWING PAGES: At the back of the home, a private arcadia unfolds.

Order, Peace, and Harmony

A landscape of summits and clouds arises on the dining room wall: *A Thousand Li of Rivers and Mountains*, inspired by a Song dynasty scroll, is hand-painted onto silk by de Gournay, representing order, peace, and harmony as a natural setting. It is wonderful symbolism for a space where two aesthetic perspectives came into balance—my husband and I acquired this home at the beginning of our journey together, in a period when we were merging our sensibilities. We wanted to create a haven, an urban sanctuary, where we could enjoy quiet and contentedness together.

Located in the Buckhead neighborhood of Atlanta, our Georgian-style flat dwells in a building designed by a protégé of architect Philip Trammell Shutze. It has old-world sensibility, via classical scale and proportions, and a charming courtyard. Inspired by an English flat I had previously in Belgravia, London, I wanted to create tailored and welcoming rooms. My husband and I were also inspired by The Lowell, the historic, circa 1927 hotel where we stay on our frequent visits to New York City. Originally home to private apartments, The Lowell has been superbly and graciously updated, and its intimate, well-appointed spaces hold so many fond memories for us that we wanted to bring its spirit home.

Very little needed to be done to the flat structurally, because the original interior architecture was classical perfection. We did extensively renovate the kitchen and baths, working closely with craftspeople and metalworkers to create spaces precisely engineered to meet our needs. Iron-and-marble open shelving anchors the kitchen, and I love the dynamism of black and white.

PAGE 252: A granite bust of Beethoven by French sculptor Honoré Sausse was discovered at Gerald Bland. PREVIOUS PAGES: In the dining room we gather with friends around the mahogany English tilt-top breakfast table, illuminated by a circa 1800 Russian Empire gilt bronze and crystal chandelier. Beethoven rests upon a circa 1820 pier table attributed to Duncan Phyfe. OPPOSITE: Chinese immortals grace the black-lacquer shelving. PAGES 258 AND 259: Above the fireplace mantel is a composition of lustrous patinated pieces and a drawing by Danish artist Louise Fenne.

PREVIOUS PAGES: The living room, with its elegant balance and tailored sophistication, was inspired by our favorite hotel in New York, The Lowell. ABOVE, LEFT TO RIGHT: Deep bordeaux cosmos are a poetic presence. So is Buddha, who centers a composition in cloud colors of gray and white. The bar is home to a William Trost Richards landscape of Mullion Cove in Cornwall, England, which holds a special place in the history of my family. An intimate corner in the kitchen keeping room—a delightful place to be ensconced during the day.

As an art student, I learned that when creating a composition, negative space is as important as positive. This home is a case study of that philosophy. With pale walls that are an extension of the clouds in the Chinese landscape and fabrics the color of pearls, there is space for the eye to rest. Against this ethereal backdrop, fine antiques—a convex girandole glass mirror, a nineteenth-century gilt-wood console, bronze French sconces—are dazzling. In the dining room, a bust of Beethoven by Honoré Sausse, in dark and sonorous granite, stands out against the cream-hued wall, providing a moment of high drama.

Collecting antiques is a passion I share with my husband. Before we met, he had acquired an extraordinary collection of fine Federal furniture, and we built on that together, seeking antiques across the globe. Among our favorite pieces, a nineteenth-century mahogany tilt-top English breakfast table, and a circa 1820 Philadelphia gilt-wood console with a dashing eagle that greets our guests in the foyer.

We incorporated many works from my personal collections of art and objects as well. In the living room, a drawing by Louise Fenne graces the mantel, and over the bar hangs a William Trost Richards landscape, inherited from my grandfather, of Mullion Cove in Cornwall, England. On the black-lacquer shelves, carvings of eight Chinese immortals, discovered in Hong Kong by a great-aunt, appear to hover above their glass risers.

A well-designed home should tell your story. This pied-à-terre narrates our collective journey as a couple.

OPPOSITE: We renovated the kitchen down to the last meticulous detail, and cast it in my favorite palette, black and white. The iron open shelving visually anchors the space.

ABOVE, LEFT TO RIGHT: The handsome bath is fitted with black Nero Marquina marble. The primary bedroom diaphanously dressed in cream-and-white embroidered textiles is a dream. The grisaille wallcovering in the bath is the backdrop for a nineteenth-century academic figure drawing. A bold, black door punctuates the haven of the bath.

OPPOSITE AND ABOVE: The refined, monochromatic space features a dressing table topped with beloved photos and treasured family heirlooms.

Sanctuary

In his reflections on interior space, French philosopher Gaston Bachelard wrote of the miniature, "A tiny door opens a world." This Brays Island cottage—at a petite 1,400 square feet—is a powerful portal for both heart and home. My clients developed the property as a guesthouse for a subsequent larger home, and the charming cottage became a beloved place of sanctuary for family and friends.

The owners named the property, sited on a single acre of land, Little Lodge. The word "lodge" has its origins in the French *loge*, meaning "arbor," and indeed the house is surrounded by a field of green and sheltered by southern live oaks. The roof rises like a steeple out of this arcadia, its striking silhouette delightfully unexpected in the Lowcountry landscape.

Designed by architect Peter Block and built by the inspired owner, the home is a model of the new old house. It is rooted in Arts and Crafts tradition and the work of late nineteenth-century and early twentieth-century English architects C. F. A. Voysey and Edwin Lutyens. Many métiers contributed to its creation; among the bespoke elements are hand-fired and hand-laid clinker bricks and honed Belgian bluestone.

The interiors needed to unfold as gracefully as the house itself. We composed the rooms to be comfortable and inviting, the furnishings to be in relaxed conversation with each other. In the living room, a wool sofa and a leather ottoman

PAGE 270: With its picturesque arches of hand-fired clinker-brick, the entry has the romanticism of an English country house. OPPOSITE: The vestibule also functions as a boot room, a nod to the sporting locale.

commune with polished pieces like a French walnut buffet and antique iron lanterns. The primary bedroom and bath are serene refuges, the former enveloped in muted fabrics, the latter clad in white marble.

I believe that nature is the true sanctuary, so our design here has roots in the landscape. For the dining room we commissioned a pastoral mural of nearby marshlands by Savannah artist Bob Christian that makes the wall feel as if it disappears into the fog that so often settles in Lowcountry. In the kitchen there is a feeling of a conservatory—the room is transparent to the trees and awash in light due to the soaring verticality of Peter's design—and we enhanced the sunlit atmosphere with a palette of pale wood finishes on the cabinetry. And at the very top of the house, we wrapped a bedroom nested beneath the curve of the eave, called the Treehouse Room, in a faux-bois wallcovering. Sleeping here is like sleeping in the arms of an ancient oak.

Our visiting family now often stay in this home. They settle into Little Lodge the week before Christmas, when the clients holiday elsewhere. The house sits next to a pasture where horses graze; the grandchildren run out and stand on the fence rails with carrots. We have a wonderful picture of three of the boys doing just that—a wonderful memento of this place in our hearts.

PREVIOUS PAGES: A custom mural by Savannah artist Bob Christian inspired by the home's Lowcountry setting serves as the focal point for the entire space. A pair of antique English lanterns cast a glow over the scene. OPPOSITE: Flowing from the dining room, the living room, dubbed the Storytelling Room by the client, encourages the telling of tall tales over after-dinner drinks.

ABOVE: Even though the home is of small scale, the height of the windows makes it feel spacious. OPPOSITE: Exquisite pale gray hues and linen bask in the lovely light of the primary bedroom.

OPPOSITE: The bunk room, referred to fondly as the Treehouse Room, is tucked under the eaves and wrapped in faux-bois wallcovering.
ABOVE: With its creamy palette, the guest bath is an exercise in simplicity.

ABOVE: The glorious kitchen has the feel of a conservatory. The architect's sculptural, ogee soapstone backsplash gives the room additional flair and material richness. OPPOSITE: Ascendant floor-to-ceiling windows and the wood grain of the cabinetry underscore the verticality of the space. FOLLOWING PAGES: Little Lodge nestles into its lush, green, pastoral world.

Acknowledgments

"Real elegance is everywhere—especially in the things that don't show."
—*Christian Dior*

Standing before Manet's *Le Dejeuner sur l'herbe* at the Musée d'Orsay, I am transported. I experience a quickening of the spirit that stills time, that dissolves even a place of this scale and grandeur. I feel this, too, in the presence of an exquisite ikebana or a delicate piece of creamware. We are momentarily released, elevated in spirit, by visual beauty.

Yet I am most enduringly lifted by the invisible embrace of those I am fortunate to call family, friends, and colleagues. I am eternally grateful for their depth of care, dedication, artistry, and support; for the companionship and joie de vivre of my global community of art, architecture, and design; for the trust and vision of my extraordinary clients; for the creativity and mastery of the artists and craftspeople with whom I get to embark on soul-enriching collaborations. The world of interiors is a channel for all of these graces.

I've always been immensely grateful for the certainty of my calling, of the vision for the trajectory of my life. Whether we are designing interiors and furnishings, curating art, choreographing a tabletop, or tending to a garden, we are cultivating a life. Creating happy homes—places of warmth, harmony, intimacy, peace—that is the impetus for all I do.

Embracing me always are . . .

My beloved husband Chuck, my darling children and grandchildren, and, of course, our dog, Biscuit.

Our exceptional clients, with whom we get to embark on the magical journey to home, and beyond.

My phenomenally talented book partners at Rizzoli, Charles Miers and Kathleen Jayes. Jill Cohen and Lizzy Hyland, who shepherded this project to fruition so beautifully. Our designers, Doug Turshen, Steve Turner, and John Lineweaver, who bless me with their creative guidance, and extraordinary writer and poet Alisa Carroll.

My esteemed advisor and confidante extraordinaire, Laurie Salmore.

The brilliant publications editors who have so graciously supported our work and given it such gorgeous context.

My studio team both past and present to whom I offer my undying gratitude: Amy Ely, Kate Bruno, Wynne Davis, Leslie Keating Nalewaik, Mary Ellen Jones, and Caroline Miller.

Our other collaborators: Beth Ault, Jennifer Orne, and Lane Smith.

Our wonderful NivenBreen team: Ellen Niven, Chesie Breen, and Sydney Wallace.

A home is a collaborative endeavor, and I'm forever grateful for the breadth and depth of knowledge of the talented architects, builders, landscape architects, artists, craftspeople, workrooms, and vendors who help us bring these projects to life.

We dedicate our lives, very intentionally, to designing beautiful, meaningful, and comforting homes for our clients. I hope you, too, feel held by the beauty, seen and unseen, that surrounds you.

Project Credits

A PLACE OF TRANQUILITY AND GRACE

ARCHITECT: D. Stanley Dixon Architects

PROJECT ARCHITECT: Clark Templeton

PROJECT TEAM: Kate Bruno, Wynne Davis, Rachel Samaras Gavalas, and Coley Loudermilk

BUILDER: Purvis Builders

LANDSCAPE ARCHITECT: Stephen W. Hackney

PHOTOGRAPHER: Lisa Romerein Photography

LANDSCAPE PHOTOGRAPHER: Neil Landino

STYLIST: Eleanor Roper Interior Style and Design

OUTSIDE OF TIME

ARCHITECT: Choate + Hertlein Architects

BUILDER: Gray Hanavich

PHOTOGRAPHER: Lisa Romerein Photography

STYLIST: Eleanor Roper Interior Style and Design

COASTAL LIGHT

ARCHITECT: T.S. Adams Studio, Architects

PROJECT ARCHITECT: Paul Geary

PROJECT TEAM: Mary Clare Holm, Colby Walker, Courtney Mellott, and Frances Jackson

BUILDER: Davis Dunn Construction

LANDSCAPE ARCHITECT: Land Plus

PHOTOGRAPHER: Lisa Romerein Photography

STYLIST: Eleanor Roper Interior Style and Design

A GROUNDED SPIRIT

ARCHITECT: Jeffrey Dungan Architects

PROJECT ARCHITECT: Emily Schmidt

PROJECT TEAM: Tristan Harstan, Maya Foldes, Sarah Riddle, and Leah Myers

BUILDER: TCC Construction

LANDSCAPE ARCHITECT: Agricultural Services

PHOTOGRAPHER: William Abranowicz

STYLIST: Eleanor Roper Interior Style and Design

A DREAM THE SEA MAKES

ARCHITECT: Harrison Design

PROJECT ARCHITECT: Chad Goehring

PROJECT TEAM: Mary Clare Holm, Courtney Mellott, and Colby Walker

BUILDER: B.C. Construction

LANDSCAPE ARCHITECT: Sea Island Landscape

PHOTOGRAPHER: Emily Followill Photography

STYLIST: Eleanor Roper Interior Style and Design

SOLIDITY AND STRENGTH

ARCHITECT: Vera Iconica Architecture

PROJECT ARCHITECT: Chris Hancock

PROJECT TEAM: Amy Ely, Kimberly Coleman, and Maria Dominguez

BUILDER: Dembergh Construction

LANDSCAPE ARCHITECT: Mark Herschberger at Herschberger Design

PHOTOGRAPHER: William Abranowicz

STYLIST: Eleanor Roper Interior Style and Design

A STUDY IN CLARITY

ARCHITECT: Jeffrey Dungan Architects

PROJECT ARCHITECT: Joel Solomon

BUILDER: Gulf View Construction

LANDSCAPE ARCHITECT: Agricultural Services

PHOTOGRAPHER: William Abranowicz

A STORYBOOK MADE REAL

ARCHITECT: D. Stanley Dixon Architects

PROJECT ARCHITECT: Clark Templeton

PROJECT TEAM: Tristan Harstan, Maya Foldes, Leah Myers, and Sarah Riddle

BUILDER: Russ Cooper Associates

LANDSCAPE ARCHITECT: Glenn Gardiner

PHOTOGRAPHER: Eric Piasecki Photography

STYLIST: Helen Crowther

CREATIVITY IN DIALOGUE

ARCHITECT: Peter Block Architects

PROJECT ARCHITECT: Richard Burgess

PROJECT TEAM: Amy Ely and Kimberly Coleman

BUILDER: Derazi Homes

LANDSCAPE ARCHITECT: Floralis Garden Design

PHOTOGRAPHER: Lisa Romerein Photography

STYLIST: Eleanor Roper Interior Style and Design

ELEGANCE AND REPOSE

ARCHITECT: Summerour Architects

PROJECT TEAM: Amy Ely, Rahela Crawford, and Cole Beckwith Bishop

BUILDER: Derazi Homes

LANDSCAPE ARCHITECT: Planters

PHOTOGRAPHER: Lisa Romerein Photography

STYLIST: Helen Crowther

ORDER, PEACE, AND HARMONY

ARCHITECT: Tucker and Howell

PROJECT TEAM: Amy Ely

PHOTOGRAPHER: Lisa Romerein Photography

STYLIST: Eleanor Roper Interior Style and Design

SANCTUARY

ARCHITECT: Peter Block Architects

PROJECT TEAM: Mary Clare Holm, Colby Walker, and Kate Fleming

BUILDER: Young & Meathe

PHOTOGRAPHER: Emily Followill Photography

STYLIST: Eleanor Roper Interior Style and Design

First published in the United States of America in 2025 by
Rizzoli International Publications, Inc.
49 West 27th Street
New York, NY 10001
www.rizzoliusa.com

Copyright © 2025 Beth Webb
Text: Beth Webb and Alisa Carroll

PHOTO CREDITS:
William Abranowicz: front cover, case, 2-3, 92-109, 126-151, 153-167

Emily Followill: 5, 8, 110-125, 270-285

Francesco Lagnese: 46

Neil Landino: 44-45

Eric Piasecki: 168-201

Lisa Romerein: back cover, endpapers, 6, 11, 13-43, 48-91, 202-269

ART CREDITS:
Page 29: Henri Matisse, Florentine, 1938 © 2024 Succession H. Matisse / Artists Rights Society (ARS), New York

Pablo Picasso, Oiseau No. 82, 1963 © 2024 Estate of Pablo Picasso / Artists Rights Society (ARS), New York

Endpapers: Maysey Craddock, *Vessel for a Rising Sun*, 2022

Case: Chris Condon, *Flyway*, 2021

Front cover: Sabine Maes, *Helene*, 2021

Back cover: Pablo Picasso, Oiseau No. 82, 1963 © 2024 Estate of Pablo Picasso / Artists Rights Society (ARS), New York

Henri Matisse, Florentine, 1938 © 2024 Succession H. Matisse / Artists Rights Society (ARS), New York

All rights reserved. No part of this publication may be reproduced, stored in a retrieval system, or transmitted in any form or by any means, electronic, mechanical, photocopying, recording, or otherwise, without prior consent of the publishers.

Publisher: Charles Miers
Senior Editor: Kathleen Jayes
Design: Doug Turshen with Steve Turner
Production Manager: Rebecca Ambrose
Managing Editor: Lynn Scrabis

Developed in collaboration with Jill Cohen Associates

ISBN: 978-08478-2991-0
Library of Congress Control Number: 2024945608

Printed in Italy
2025 2026 2027 2028 / 10 9 8 7 6 5 4 3 2 1

Visit us online:
Instagram.com/RizzoliBooks
Facebook.com/RizzoliNewYork
X: @Rizzoli_Books
Youtube.com/user/RizzoliNY

FRONT COVER: *Helene* by Sabine Maes (2021) in a Jackson Hole, Wyoming, residence. ENDPAPERS: Detail of *Vessel for a Rising Sun* (2022) by Maysey Craddock. Gouache, thread, and flashe on found paper. PAGE 1: A silhouette of *Serenity*, a 1947 green Maine granite sculpture by William Zorach, in the living room of a Tennessee residence. PAGES 2-3: The monastic aura of the living room in our project in Jackson Hole. DEDICATION: On St. Simons Island, the elegant simplicity of the foyer. CONTENTS: An evocative studded wooden bowl accessorizes a tabletop in a California beach house. INTRODUCTION: A graceful vignette in the living room of our St. Simons Island project. In the Tennessee home, a luminous bar alcove. BACK COVER: In this serene, sophisticated keeping room, each element stands like sculpture in an edited composition. The focal art installation features *Oiseau No. 82* (1963), a Picasso ceramic; *Florentine* (1938), a linocut by Matisse; and *Hummingbird* (2022), a work on paper by contemporary artist Shelley Reed. CASE: *Flyway* (2021), a series of individual, hand-carved wooden birds by sculptor Chris Condon, takes flight in the Jackson Hole project.